MINIATURE SHETLAND PONY

"My For Reals Story"

Written By Azlanna Coote

DEDICATION

I has to say a very big thank you to Debbie Docborough for saving me and finding me my forevers home. I will never forgets you or what you dids for me.

I would also likes to says a big thank you to Dr. Roisin Wood for takings the bestest care of me and helpings me to gets better, even though she gives me the prickly sticks. Loves you both!

CONTENTS

To alls my lovely friends on the Facebook for your loves and supports, which has helpsed me gets through my opserations. I loves you more than words cans says.

PREFACE

When I was a child, I dreamed of horses, especially Black Beauty, as it was a series on the television at the time. I became besotted with horses and I would have done anything to have one of my very own.

We didn't have very much growing up and I lived in town, so unfortunately I couldn't get near any horses, but I never gave up on my dream. Who knew that my Black Beauty would come along later in life in a wonderful little bundle called Jasper. He is everything I dreamed of, although a lot smaller than I imagined. He is beautiful, funny, mischievous and so full of character, but I think it's his courage that I admire most of all.

Jasper really suffered neglect and abuse before being rescued and if that wasn't enough, he has had to endure painful operations because of his bone deformities. What amazes me about him, is he hasn't let these negative experiences affect his personality. He loves people, which is a miracle considering the abuse he suffered and he faces everything without fear or mistrust.

Jasper inspires me every day. The love I have for him and he for me has changed me forever. I feel so blessed that he came into my life.

Thank you for purchasing this book, all the profits will be going towards his forthcoming operation and ongoing medical care.

Azlanna Coote

CHAPTER 1

My name is Jasper, although I also gets called naughty pickle, quites a lot actually, now I comes to think about it. I'm not very good at being told whats to do, which is probably why I gets into trouble all the times. I don't thinks I am naughty exactly, I just haves very strong opinions abouts things, especially carrots. I loves the carrots. Where was I? Oh yes! I am a Miniature Shetland Pony and I am going to tell you how I gots rescued. You won't believes what has happened to me already and I am only three. I have almost been shot, eaten by angry woofa's, been on two boats, broked my shoulder, had wonky legs problems and been in hospital. TWICE!! I can only write in Jasper speak though, because, well I'm me and you must remembers that hooman isn't my first language. So my hooman, who I call Mum, loves her, has written the hooman words for the Jasper speaks at the back of this book, in case you gets stuck.

Lets me start my story by telling you that I live in the Jersey with two other ponies, Teddy whose seventeen, he is ginger and has the wilds hair. He is a Shetland too, but he is normals size, so a lots taller than me. He has weirdy eyes, one is blue and one is brown. Mokey is two, he is brown with white patches, although he says he is white with brown patches. It's his furs, so I guesses he knows what colour he is.

I also has a small woofa called Snoopy, which gives me the fusions because he is a Jack Russel. If he is a Jack, why is he called Snoopy? I also has a bunny called Buddy, who lives with me in my stable and a birdie that has sort of moved in with Teddy. He thinks he is invisibles to hoomans by the way, but that is a whole other story. We just calls him Birdie.

Now, this is my forevers home, but that's not where my story starts, no! It actually starts in Wales with my mother. I wasn't with her very long because I was a bit of a surprise to her hoomans. When they bought her, they didn't knows I was in her tummy. That's probably on accounts of us Shetlands being very hairy and round. Anyways, as soon as I poppsed out, they tried to sells me, but nobody wanted me cans you believes? So you will never guess what they did? They sent me offs to a market. I didn't knows what that was at the time because I was only six months old, but I do remembers my mother being full of the upsets and the worries. She tries to helps me understands what would happen to me, but I didn't really listen. I am easily distracted apparently. To be honests, I don't thinks I knew what was happening. All I cared about was eating and lets me tells you, nothing much has changed there.

You would thinks all of this would have been very scary for me, especially being sent away from my mother, but you know, I am not really afeared of things. In fact, I loves adventures. So on the day I hads to go, I was totally fine abouts it and I wents quite happily onto the lorry. Didn't like seeing my mother sad though. I kept tellings her I would be fine, but she wasn't havings it at all. She caused a right ruckus.

It was a bit bumpy in the lorry, but thanks the goodness, it wasn't a very long trip. I could hears the market even before we gots there. There were lots of hoomans shouting and I haves to say, the horses were just as noisy. When the lorry doors opened up, all I could see was busyness. Horses and ponies walksing up and down and hoomans everywhere. The market was not at all what I expected. I has never beens to a market, so I don't knows what I was expectings really. A large hooman, that smelled a bits funny, came onto the lorry and putted a rope on me and leds me off.

"Hello, my name is Jasper, pleased to meets you," I said to every horse and pony I passed. Nothing! Not one horse or pony spoked to me. There were hoomans shouting and some were grabbing ponies heads and looking at their teeths. Very rude I thoughts and what were they looking for in there? All the way up the path were lots of little grassy patches with shiny metal rails around them. The hooman took me over to a grassy patch and shoved me in.

"Ooohl Grass," I said to myself. Loves the grass more than anything, so I hads to taste it and I was feeling very hungry after my trip. When my tummy felt full, I looked up to see what was going on and I noticed that there was a brown pony, bigger thans me, on my right hoof side and an even bigger black and white pony on my left.

"Hello," I said. "My name is Jasper." Still nothing, maybe they don't speaks Jasper in the markets. They both ignoreds me and just stared into the crowd of noisy hoomans. The pony on my right was taken out of his grassy patch and he gots all skitsy. The hooman growled at him and gave him a sharps tug on his rope and dragged him offs.

"Your next," said the other pony.

I nearly jumped out of my fur with the shocks. A pony spoked to me!

"Next for whats?" I said.

She didn't answer. Not going to lie, I started to feel flutterflies in my tummy at that point. This wasn't as funs as I thought it was going to be. In facts, I just wanted to be back home with my mother. I had hads enough excitement for one day. I decided to asks the next hooman that cames past, if they could please puts me back on the lorry and takes me home.

"Excuse me, can you takes me home now please?" I said. They just ignoreds me and left me there. Well my turn came quite quickly after that and a large hooman with fur on his face, putted a rope on me and pulled me out of my patch, rather roughly I must say.

After seeing what happened to the other pony, I cided to walks out nicely. He took me into a big open circle that was totally surrounded by hoomans, who were all staring at me and muttering to themselfs.

"Hello everybody," I said with my bestest smiley face. There was a man shouting out to all the hoomans and then before I had times to say anything else, I was taken back to my grassy patch. The pony next to me shook her head.

"I am so sorry, such a youngin too," she said.

"Why are you sorries?" I asked.

She looked at me with the sad eyes. "You didn't get sold."

"I didn't? How do you knows? What does that means?" I said.

This was all very fusing.

"Nothing good happens to a pony that doesn't get sold," she said.

Before I could asks her more, she was taken out of her patch and that was the last I saw of her. I stood for the rest of the day on my own feeling a bit lonely and afeared. By the time someone came to gets me, the sun was going down and it was getting rather chilly. I was very pleased to see the hooman coming towards me and I really hoped I was going to get something nice to eats. He had the grumps though and just putted a rope on me and took me off to another very big lorry, which wasn't the one I cames on. There were four other ponies in this lorry, all a lots bigger than me. I was the lasts to be put on because I was the smallest. It was very quiet in the lorry, so I thoughts I should says something.

"Hello! Are you coming home with me?" I said as friendly as I could. None of thems answered me. I tried my hardests to stay standings up, but it was so wobbly in the lorry. I accidently fell hard on the floppy wall that separated me and a very large pony. He just glareds down at me with the fiercest face I have ever seed, which freaksed me right outs. I really wanted to go home to my mother and my very own grassy patch. I cided then and there, that maybe adventures wasn't for me after alls. I was stucks in that lorry for the longest time and after a whiles, I started to falls asleep. I didn't wakes up until the noisy lorry came to a very hard stop, which made us all falls sideways. I could hear angry woofa's and there was really bad smells coming from outside.

Before I hads time to ask where we were, the big door of the lorry opened up. It was dark now and the woofa's next to a very sewious, grumpy looksing hooman were going bonkers. They had very hungry looks in their eyes that gave me the uneasies. Well, I wasn't home that was for sure. I couldn't see much on accounts of the darkness, but I could see lots of wet, muddy ground, everywhere.

The grumpy hooman grabbed me and draggeds me off the lorry, so roughly I nearly felled over. I only have little legs and I am not good at walking down slopes. He gots the frustrations with me and carries me out by my front legs, which really hurted. Then he droppsed me and pushed me into a muddy patch with some other ponies and a very big horse. She looked very skinny, not round like me, actually they all looked very skinny.

"Hello, I'm Jasper," I said. Well, she didn't give me the grumps face like all the others had, but she looked full of the sads.

"I'm Bess. Come and stand by me before you get trampled?" She said in a very kind voice.

I can't tells you how happy I was that she spoked to me because I was starting to feel a bits afeared. I went and stood right up close to her and she gaves me a little nuzzle on my neck, which really calmsed me down. I looked about to see where the grassy patch was, but there was just mud everywheres. I did spot a little bits of hay in the middle, but all the other ponies were eating it all ups and when I tried to joins them, they showed me their teeths and they even bucksed at me.

"Get out of it!" said a very nasty looking grey pony.

I trotted back over to Bess and hids under her tummy.

"Don't worry Jasper, I will get you some hay in the morning, but there won't be much. You are going to get very hungry," she said.

I didn't like the sounds of that, so I started to feel the upsets. I was hungry, tired and missing my mother. I stayed close to Bess and managed to shut my eyes. I was so tired, I didn't wakes up until the sun cames up the next morning.

At first I forgots where I was and I woked up all happy, but then I saw the muddy patch we were on and even worserer than that, no grass or hay! A funny rumbly noise came from my tummy.

"Excuse me," I said to Bess. "Where is the grass?"

She looked at me with a kind face. "There isn't any. The farmer will drop a bit of hay in later, if we are lucky. You need to toughen up little one and get to it first with me, otherwise you will starve."

"I don't understands. Why am I here and why is there no foods?" I said.

"You are here because no one wanted you, so you were given to the farmer. He gets all the unwanted horses and ponies from the market. I was sent there because I got old. I did everything my hoomans wanted over the years, but it wasn't enough," she said sadly.

"Well, that's not nice is it? My hoomans didn't want me eithers. So why doesn't the farmer hooman feeds us and why don't we haves a grassy patch?" I said.

Bess just looked out over the fields and said nothing. Before I hads the time to ask more questions, the farmer cames over and droppsed some hay over the fence. Bess charged over with the fierceness.

"Jasper, quick now, as fast as you can," she shouted.

It was food, I didn't needs to be asked twice. One thing you will learns about me is, I likes my foods. I gallopsed over and started munching as quickly as I could. Even though it was a bit wets and smelled funny, it tasted so goods.

I could see Bess bucksing and biting the other ponies. If I didn't knows her already, she would have given me the big frights. One of the bigger ponies gaves her a nasty bite on her shoulder and red stuff starting leaksing out. She gaves out a big squeal and an almighty buck, getting the nasty pony right in his chest. Bess then quickly cames over to me and ated a bit of hay.

"Jasper, go now," she shouted.

Now, I knows I should have done as I was told, but I was so hungry and I did says, I am not very good at the listening. I looked up, Bess was gone and all I seed was a row of teeths coming at me. You might not knows this, but us Shetland ponies might be little, but we are really quicks. I moved so fast, you wouldn't believes it. I gallopsed over to Bess and hids under her tummy again, which was making lots of growling noises.

The days seemed to go on forever and the night times were cold and lonely. Thanks the goodness, I had Bess to looks after me because I thinks the other ponies would have eated me or squished me into the muddy patch. I have gots to say, it didn't takes long for my round tummy to disappear.

I was very tired, so when the monsooning and the hooley blew in, I thoughts I would falls over. I really had the miseries and poor Bess wasn't well at all, so she couldn't helps me get the hay anymore. I hads to use my smarts. So I watched for the farmer hooman and I mades sure, I was quicker than the others gettings to the hay he threwed in. I would eats as fast as I could, grabs a bit for Bess and takes it over to her.

"Bess, what is going to happens to me? I don't like it here at all and I wants to go home," I said. Bess, didn't speak at first, but then she said it.

"Jasper, we won't be here much longer. Have you noticed the farmer taking a pony out every now and then?" she said.

"Actually, I haves. Where did they goes?" I said, hoping it was to a nice grassy patch.

"They go into the barn over there and they don't come out."

I looked over at the barn and thoughts about it. "Well what's in there?"

"Nothing good Jasper. Nothing good. Just know if you go in there, you won't be coming out," she said with lots of sadness in her eyes.

I swalloweds hard and I felts very cold alls of a sudden. "I don't thinks I will go in there."

"If the farmer comes for you Jasper, as soon as you get past the fence, you buck, you pull, you bite and you gallop as fast as you can. Your only hope is to escape."

Well that's what I will do, I thoughts. I didn't want to talks anymore, it was getting dark and cold, so I just snugglesed up as close as I coulds to Bess.

The next morning I was woken ups by a car and a very cross lady hooman shoutings at the farmer. The farmer didn't looks happy at all and actually he seemed a bit afeared of the lady hooman. There were arms waving and lots of the arguments. She was pointing over at me, whilst she was shoutings at the farmer. Then it was all over and she gots back into her car and droves off. Normally I would have wanted to knows what all the fusses was abouts, but Bess and me were really starting to feel the sickness and we couldn't even moves to gets the hay when it arriveds. The sticky ground was so deeps now, I didn't have the strengths to walk through it. We just sleepsed all day.

That night when the darkness cames and we were all settleds in for a very wet, cold night, the farmer hooman droved his lorry right up to our patch and he lowered the big door. He opened the gate and grabbed me before I hads times to do anything. I wanted to escapes just likes Bess tolds me, but I was so hungry and tired, I hads no bucks in me and neither did Bess. In fact we coulds hardly walks now. He just draggeds us both out and putted us on the lorry.

The big door closed behinds us and off we wents. I had no idea where we was going and I didn't really cares anymore. I just laids down and went to sleeps. I was so tired, I think I coulds have sleepsed forevers. In

14

facts, I was still asleeps when the lorry stopped. I didn't opens my eyes until I heard a hooman talksing to me and I looked up to sees very kind eyes.

"You're not the nasty farmer," I said sleepily. He carried on talksing to me whilst he picked me up and carried me gently across a yard into a large wooden house.

The nice hooman laid me down on some fluffy stuff and gave me a big pile of hay.

I couldn't stands up, but I coulds still eats. Did I eats!! I can't tells you how happy I was to have a big pile of hay alls to myselfs at last. I was so busy with the eatings, I didn't notice the lady hooman comes into my stable and sit next to me. She was givings me lots of pats. It was the same lady hooman, that I had seeds this morning arguing with the nasty farmer.

"Now don't you worry little man, you are safe now and I am going to get you all fixed up," she said givings me the biggest kiss on my nose.

I wasn't really listening, all I could hear was my tummy grumbling with the shocks at the foods going in. I was already feelings much better.

The next day was lovely and sunny, so I was ables to haves a good looks about. I was in a big wooden house with my owns little stable. There was another horse and pony in the house withs me and thanks the goodness, so was Bess.

"Where are we Bess?" Do you know what's happening?" I said, so pleased to see her.

"We have been rescued Jasper, by a hooman called Debbie. Just in time too because he was getting ready to shoot us," she said so easily.

My mouth dropped open and a big bit of hay felled outs. "We was going to be shooted!" I couldn't quite believes my ears.

"I have seen hoomans do that to the bunnies near where I used to lives." I said. "Thanks the goodness Debbie rescued us."

Just as we ended our sation, Debbie cames into my stable. My fur was all tangly with the thorny bits, so she sats next to me and cutted thems all out. I hads a good brush and then she tooks me out to a nice big grassy patch. I couldn't believes my eyes. The sun was out and there was lots of lovely grass to eats. I hads a good roll and then I just eated and eated.

CHAPTER 2

Not goings to lie, it tooks a longs time for me to gets my strengths back. I can't believes how skinny I gots, but luckily Debbie took greats care of me and gaves me so much loves. She also gaves me my very first carrot, best thing I has ever tasted. Carrots are my most favourites thing in the whole worlds. I quickly forgots about the horribles time I hads. I don't likes to thinks about it. "Don't keeps looking backwards, otherwise it messes up your forwards," that's what I always says.

Life on this farm was happy and fun. There were lots of other ponies to play with and of course Bess, my favourites, on accounts of how she looksed after me in the place we won't talks about. Loves Bess! I knew this wasn't my forevers home because the other ponies tolds me. They said Debbie rescues ponies like me, then she searches for the prefect homes for them all. I thoughts I was happy with that, until she found Bess a new home. Of course, I was so happy for her, but I felts the sadness right downs in my tummy. Bess couldn't quite believes that someone would wants an old horse like her, but the lady hooman that cames to see her had a kind face, so we both knew she would be fines.

The night before she left, we stayed up talksing all night long, much to the annoyances of the other ponies.

"Is you excited to go to your new home Bess?" I asked, whilst munching on my hay.

"Yes, but I am a bit scared in case they change their mind like all the other hoomans have. I can't end up in that market again. I won't survive Jasper," she said.

"Debbie would never lets that happen, I knows she wouldn't. She tolds me that I will stays with her as long as it takes to find the perfect home for me and I trusts her. You have gots to believes in Debbie," I said.

"You're right Jasper. You are really smart for such a young pony," she said with a chuckle.

"I knows, everybody keeps tellings me," I said. I thinks I grewed a bit just then.

Bess left quite soon after thats and I thoughts I would be full of the sads, but then Ginger trotted into my life. Ginger was the most beautiful filly pony, I hads ever seens and she was the same age as me. Well, she really brought the naughty pickle out in me and I thinks I drove poor Debbie bonkers. I did everything I coulds to get over the fence and into her grassy patch. Ginger wasn't that pleased about my antiques either, but the more she bucksed at me and told me she didn't likes me, the more I chased after her.

I gots through the fences, quite a few times, prouds of that actually. Debbie said it was my all moans. Apparently, it's a sickness that comes to all colts. I gots to show Ginger all my stallions moves, which mades her gives me a few good kicks, but I thinks that just meant she loveds me.

Debbie hads to put me in sorry tree confinesment because she saids my all moans were turning me into a little hoodigan. My mission everyday was to gets in with the fillies, much to everyones annoyances. The only thing that tooks my minds off of Ginger and the other fillies was food and the sheeps. I discovered I really loves the sheeps. They looks so cuddly and they talks funny. They seemed to really likes me too, which I thinks was because I was the same size as thems. I spent a lot of times playing with the sheeps and I especially liked it when the baby sheeps came. Very bouncy baby sheeps are.

I spended a lovely year with Debbie and she really did keeps her promise to me because she finally founds me a forevers home in the Jersey. I hads no idea whats or wheres that was, but she said its beautiful and the hoomans were just rights for me. I was really quites excited, but I hads a bit of the worries too. After alls, the last times I went on an adventure, it

21

didn't turns out very well did it? Debbie tolds me that she searched long and hards for my forevers family, so I thoughts, if she dids that, then these hoomans must be good, mustn't they?

Me leaving was the talks of the grassy patches, especially with Ginger. Something tolds me though, she wasn't sads to see me and my all moans go, nor were the others. The only ones who seemed sads abouts it, were the sheeps and Debbie of courses.

The following morning a big lorry arrived and that was it. Debbie cames to gets me and leaded me out of my stable. Then she stopped and bent down to speaks to me.

"Now my little man, you look after yourself and be happy," she said.

I could see she hads the upsets, so I gaves her a big kiss and a cuddle to says a big thank you for savings me. Then I holded my muzzle up high and I trotted onto that lorry as proud as cans be.

"Bye Ginger! Bye sheeps! Bye everybody!" I said as I went in. Only the sheeps shouted goodbye back. Very rudes I thoughts.

So far all my trips in the lorries hads been quite short, but this trip went on and on and on. I had hay this times though, so that was good. Only me in the lorry too, which was a bits lonely. It was nearly dark when I arriveds at the next stop. I could just about sees lots of grassy patches and very smart looking stables with very big horses in them. You shoulds have seeds their faces when I gots off the lorry and walksed towards them. Great big horses they were and mosts of them had the panics.

"What is it?" I heard one says.

"Is it a woofa?" another one asked.

A woofa, can you believes it? Big horses are so stupids me thinks.

"Hello everybody, my name is Jasper and no, I am nots a woofa, I am a Miniature Shetland Pony," I shouted proudly as I walksed past. It all went very quiets and they all just stared at me. The quietness and all the eyes starings at me, mades my tummy gets the flutterflies. The very nice hooman who tooks me off the lorry, walksed me into a lovely stable with a pile of hay. As soon as I saws the foods, I forgots about the weirdy horses and my flutterfly tummy. When the lights went off and the hoomans lefts to go into the big house, I tried to speaks to the horse in the next stable.

"Excuse me, coulds you tell me if this is the Jersey?" I asked politely.

This very big, brown horse, stopped eatings his hay and stared at me before speakings.

"Nope, you will be leaving again tomorrow. I heard the hooman say your boat leaves in the afternoon," he said very slowly.

He then turned back to his hay and carried on

eatings. "My boat. What's a boat?" I asked.

"Absolutely no idea. Stop asking me questions," he said with the grumps.

I didn't bothers him again, as he was very big and I thinks he would have hads the tempers quite quickly. I didn't sleeps much eithers. I just tried to thinks what a boat was. I thoughts it might be a types of lorry. I must of fallsed asleeps because the sound of the lorry stoppsing outside our stables the next morning, woked me up. Before I had times to eats some more hay, the nice hooman who collected me from Debbie's cames in, putted a rope on me and trotted me onto the lorry again. There was another horse already in there, who was skitsy and full of the frights.

I didn't says hello, as to be quites honest with you, I think he hads lost the plot. I don't thinks he would have heared me anyways. I just stood in my section, which thanks the goodness was separate to the weirdy horse. I thinks he would have trampled me into the floor, if we hads been together. I ated my hay quietly and ignored all the ruckus alongsides me.

It was a very long trip and when we finally stopped, the noises I heards were the scariest ever. There big, howling noises and I could hears lots of lorries. When the little side door opened, I was very pleased to see the nice hooman. She gaves me some water and some more hay and tolds us we were at the boat. I could just sees out of the door and do you know what I seed? Lots of water. Not in a bucket, but a huge bigs river that had no sides. It just wents on forevers.

Thanks the goodness, the weirdy horse had calmsed down and tolds me what he could sees out of the window. My legs are too short, so I couldn't sees anything.

"What's happening? What can you sees?" I asked.

"I can see the biggest lorry, I have ever seen and it is sitting on the water. How is that possible? All the lorries and cars are driving onto it," he said.

But then the boat made this very, very loud howling, hooting sound, which sent him into the panics again and he was skitsing all over the place. I hads the feeling this was going to be a very longs trip. When we drove onto the boat, the noises got even louder and there was a lot of shouting and banging. For some reason we were rocking all over the place, made me feel a bit squeazy actually. After a whiles, I gots used to it all and I just eated my hay. Thanks the goodness, the weirdy horse did too. Believes it or not, I even managed to falls asleeps and I didn't wakes up until our nice hooman opened the side door of the lorry to says hello.

"Not long now poppets," she said.

CHAPTER 3

I heards the lorry starts up and then we were off. I thoughts we would have another long journey, but thanks the goodness, we gots where we hads to go really quicks. When the big door opened up again, all I could sees was a huge big grassy patch and two hoomans smiling up at me. I looked up at the weirdy horse, but when I seeds his freaksed face, I cided not to asks him if this was his new home or mine. A very kind hooman came onto the lorry and gaves me the big cuddles. This was my new mum, I soon scovered.

"This is your new home, my gorgeous boy," she said.

I knew straights away that I likeds her and Dad was there too. Mum handed him my lead rope and he tooks me for a nice walk on the big grassy patch to stretch my legs. I didn't says goodbye to the weirdy horse. Not going to lie, I was glad to sees the back of that horse and the lorry. In facts, if I never seed another lorry agains, I would be full of the happies.

After a bit of grass and a nice walk, Dad walksed me across the road to the big house and the stables. Well, as soon as my little feets hit the driveway to the stables, I could hears the whinnying.

"HELLO, HELLO!" Teddy shouted out.

I can't tells you how reliefed I was, to hears a friendly pony voice. Mum tooked me over and introduced me to him. I likeds him rights away, he was the same colour as ginger, only bigger and a he not a her.

"Hello, pleased to meets you," I said. Well, I has never heard a pony talks so much. He was so excited to meets me.

"Hello. Where did you come from? How old are you? What's your name? Are you staying? Come and tell me all about yourself?" He said, so fast I could hardly understands him.

There was another bigger pony next to him, who was a dark, brownie, black colour, with a white star on his face, that Mum introduced as Gizmo. He didn't seems as pleased to sees me as Teddy.

"Teddy calm down, its just a pony," he said, givings me the eyes.

"Very pleased to meets you Gizmo," I said.

He just looksed me up and down, then went back to his hay. I couldn't tell if he likeds me or not, so I thoughts I would leaves him be. Dad tooks me into my new stable, which was very nice and big, with a deep fluffy bed. I hads a good roll in it I did. The walls of our stables hads the sees through walls, so we coulds all sees each other. I likeds that, beings I am quites short. I can just abouts looks over my stable door, which had been mades smaller especially for me.

Gizmo or Gizzy, as he likeds to be called, was just staring at me alls the time. I just smiled back at him because if this was my forevers home, I needed to get alongs with everybody. It was just at that moment, that I realized, I wasn't on my owns in the stable. Can you guess what was in there with me? A bunny! The nicest, fluffiest bunny, you has ever seeds.

"I'm Buddy. Do you like bunnies?" He asked.

"I don't know," I said. "I has never met a bunny before. Actually I has met some wild bunnies, but they wouldn't talks to me. It seems I don't speaks bunny."

"I speaks pony and woofa, but not hooman," he said munching on a very tasty looking carrot.

"Wow, you are a very clever bunny," I said starings at the carrot.

Before I hads time to ask where the carrots were kepts, Teddy butted in.

"So where are you from? Why are you so small?" he asked.

I ignoreds his question about my size, as I am a bit sensitives abouts that. I tolds them all about my life and everything that had happeneds to me. You should have seeds their faces, when I tolds them about the nasty farmer and nearly beings shooted. They all thoughts I was the bravest pony they hads ever met, even Gizzy thoughts so.

The next morning Mum and Dad cames out to gives us some breakfast, with carrots! Can't tells you how happy I was to sees the carrots. They taste even better in the Jersey. She gaves me lots of the brushing, which did gives me the irritations because I wanted to goes out with the others.

I was full of the excitements, when I was finally leds out. I thinks I might haves pulled a bits. I spent the whole day out on a nice big grassy patch with Teddy and Gizzy. They likes the grass as much as me, so there wasn't much of the talksing goings on, but once my tummy was all nicely filled up, I was ready to play. For some reasons, Teddy and Gizzy weren't feelings the stallion's game and Gizzy gots really cross with me.

"Do I look like I want to play stallions?" he said, with a very grumpy voice.

"Well I don't know what a pony looks like that wants to play stallions," I said very honestly. I could see that he really didn't want to talks to me. I moved on to Teddy. "Plays with me, plays with me, come on Ted!" I said.

"Jasper, its grazing time. You can't waste the grazing time." Teddy said, with a mouthful of grass.

This did fill me with the frustrations because I really wanteds to play.

"Please, please!" I kepl asking.

Teddy gaves a big sigh and gaves in. We bucksed and gallopsed all over the grassy patch and even Gizzy cided to joins in. He can really gallops that old pony, he is twenty-six you know. I hads the bestest time, although I did gets a bit carried away with the leapsing and the rearing, which mades Gizzy gives me the biggest tellings off. I went back to my grazing, full of the annoyances. "You're not the boss of me Gizzy," I said, makings sure I was far enoughs away, so he couldn't gives me the kicks.

Now as you knows, my all moans sickness was a bits of a problem for Debbie, on accounts of me trying to gets to Ginger and the other fillies. Well, it only got worserer in the Jersey. So when Mum and Dad tooks me for a walks in the valley, I was a bits of a handful when I seeds other horses, especially the mares, that's lady horses in cases you don't knows. Something just comes over me whenever I sees one. I just forgets where I am and who I'm with. I just pulls and bucks to gets to the mares. At one point, I founds myself standing rights up in Dad's arms.

"How did I gets here?" I thoughted, when I seed Dad looksing me straight in the eyes. I gaves him the right shocks I did. For some reasons, the hoomans sitting on the horses just laugheds at me because they thinks its funny that a little pony likes me, thinks he can impresses a mare ten times bigger.

Well, Mum cided that my all moans sickness needed to be sorted, so Dr Ro, she looks after me, loves her, cames up one afternoons to fix me. I hads no idea what exactly needed the fixing or how it was going to be fixed. All I remembers, is a nasty prickly stick in my neck and then everythings went all fuzzy and I couldn't sees straight.

"Teddy! Teddy! What's happening to me?" I shouted as I felled down. My legs just disappeared underneaths me. I am not goings to lie, I didn't likes how I was feelings and it did give me the worries. After that everything wents dark.

When I started to wakes up again, I felts squeezy and fuzzy still. Dr Ro gaves me a big cuddle and tolds me I was fine and to stands up. Well, that really hurted and I remembers walksing a bits funny for a whiles. When I gots back to my stable, very carefully I might adds, Teddy had the right upsets.

"Are you alright Jasper? I thought you were gone for good? So pleased you're back! What happened?" He said all at once.

He can talks that pony, but I really likes him.

"Glad your back," said Gizzy.

Well that gave me the right shocks. "See! I knewed he would loves me in the ends," I thoughts to myselfs. Now, Mum hoped that once I had my all moans fixed, I would be more relaxed, but you knows I was still the sames, although I must admits the mares didn't appeals to me so much anymores. Don't know why really, but it didn't stops me wanting to play stallions and gallopsing about like a nutter. Mum says I am always up to the mischiefs.

It was whilst I was playing the stallions with Teddy, that I gots myself into big troubles. I was gallopsing so fast, I couldn't stops and I crashed straight into a fence and then I felts a big pain in my shoulder. I remembers just standing there with the hurts and every times I tried to walks, I got the big ouch. When Mum cames to gets me, I could hardly walks, which gaves her the right worries. She called Dr Ro up to my stable straight away and they did lots of the checks on me.

"It's my shoulder Dr. Ro," I said. She wasn't too sures, so she did some photos of it, but she said that it wasn't showing as broked. By the ways, the photos were weirdy. Dr. Ro has this machine that takes the pictures inside my furs. I kept starings at it. There I was looksing at the insides of my legs! I has never thoughts about what my inside self looks like. Let's just says, I looks better with the furs on. After thats, I had to stay in my stable and rests for the longest time.

"When are you coming out to the grassy patch again?" Teddy asked.

"I don't knows, but my shoulder isn't feeling any better," I said sadly. Everybody had the worries, especially Teddy. We had become really good friends and he didn't likes it, that I couldn't comes out to plays anymore.

"But Mum said you were coming to help me get over Honey," he said.

"Whose Honey?" I asked.

Before Teddy hads the time to answer me, Buddy butted in.

"Well I like you being in all the time because you are helping me get over Elliott?"

"Whose Honey and who is Elliott and where has they gone?" I asked full of the fusions.

Teddy and Buddy looked at each other, before either of them answered.

"You go first Buddy," Ted said.

Buddy told me that he had a brother that he lived with, but he was deaf and he had lots of the sickness. One morning not too longs ago, he just didn't wakes up.

"I was so lonely when he went away. I don't like being by myself," he said with a very sad face. "But I really like you and you have made me feel a lot better. You are not a bunny of course, but I like talking to you," he said smiling again.

"I am glads that I makes you feels better," I said proudly.

I turned to Teddy. "So who is Honey?"

Teddy told me that Honey was his very own mare, beautifuls she was by the way Teddy describes her. They even shared a stable together you know and they hads never been aparts. Mum rescued thems when they was just two years old, but they didn't haves the really bad times like me. They were just unwanted, which happens a lots to horses and ponies.

"She got the bad colics months ago," he said.

Teddy couldn't tells me anymore because he gots the upsets, so Gizzy told me the rest. Apparently, the only way to stop the pains from the colics, was for the Doctor to makes her go to sleeps forevers. Well this gaves me the big shocks. I didn't knows Doctors could makes you sleeps forevers.

"What if my shoulder doesn't gets betters, will I have to go to sleeps?" I asked, full of the worries.

Teddy got even more upset when I saids that. "I can't lose another friend. I can't, I tell you!" He shouted.

Gizzy tolds him to pull himself togethers and stop getting carried away.

"Jasper, I am sure Dr Ro will sort your shoulder and Teddy, getting in a panic isn't helping Jasper is it?" Gizzy said quite firmly.

Teddy was full of the embarrassments then and we all cided to talks about something nice, to gets us out of the depressions. I must admits, I wasn't feeling my happy self in the stable the next morning. I really wanted to goes on my grassy patch. It hads been so long, I hads forgotten what it was like to eats the grass. Mum didn't want me beings on owns in the stable thanks the goodness, so she openeds my door and sats with me in the sunshines everyday, reading me stories and talksing to me. We had brushes, cuddles and lots of scratchy massages. I can't tells you how much I loves the scratchy massages. Buddy really enjoyed all the fussings too. I really likeds those special times I hads with Mum and we really gots to know each other. She mades me realizes, how lucky a pony is if they gets a kind forevers home.

When Dr Ro comes up to checks on me again, she wasn't happy that I wasn't gettings any better. She tolds Mum, that the Jersey didn't have enough of the special machines to find out what was wrongs with me, so she said I needed to go to a hospital in the France. I hads no ideas what they were talksing about, but when I seed a lorry sitting in my grassy patch a few weeks later, I did gets the flutterflies in my tummy. Lorries didn't always take me somewhere nice and I had just gots settleds with my new family.

Mum sat next to me in my stable for a chat. "Well Jasper, you have to go on the boat again so we can fix your shoulder, but don't you worry we are going to come with you?"

I can't says I was happy abouts it, but at least Mum and Dad was coming withs me this time and even Dr. Ro was goings to meet us at the hospital, whatever that is. I am guessing it has the machines that will fix my shoulder.

The night before I hads to go, Gizzy, Teddy and Buddy stayed up chattings with me and trieds to takes my mind off the trip. I really didn't wants to go.

"What am I going to do without you Jasper?" Buddy said with the upsets.

Teddy gave Buddy the grumpy stare. "Buddy you aren't helping. Don't have the worries Jasper, you will be back soon because Mum tolds me so."

"I am a bits afeared, but I will try and be braves," I said.

I didn't gets much sleeps, I has to say. We gots up really early the next morning and Mum leaded me out to my grassy patch. I had the worries about the trip, but as soon as I seeds the grass, I forgots about everything. I just munched as much as I coulds. "Grassy patch, I can't tells you how much I has missed you," I said taking a bigs mouthful. Mum letted me stay on it all day as a specials treat, until it was times to go.

"Come on Jasper, we have to go now sweetie," Mum said.

There was a big slope up onto the lorry and it was really hards for me to walk ups it with my sore shoulder, so Dad hads to helps me up. It had a nice fluffy floor likes my bed and a huge bale of hay, which mades me very happy.

"Bye Jasper, see you soon," shouted Teddy as I got onto the lorry.

Hearing him say goodbye did gives me a bit of the upsets. I looksed at him and Gizzy on my grassy patch, as the big door slowly closed. I haven't lived here very longs, but it was my home and I loved it, which made the leavings very sads, more sads than I has ever felts before.

"Pull yourselfs together Jasper," I said to myselfs. "You have been through much worserer things than this."

CHAPTER 4

I snapsed myself out of the sads and had a good looks arounds the lorry. It was different to the others I had beens on, it had a window in the fronts, so I could sees Mum and Dad, which gaves me the great comforts. We all had the chats whilst we were goings along, which mades me feels a lot happier abouts it all. Now this lorry made my legs wobbly, which really didn't helps my bad shoulder, so I hads to find a place where I could leans up against something. I founds a nice round bit at the back, so I was ables to rest my butt on it, which gaves me the steadies. "This will do nicely," I says.

The trip to the water was very quicks and I knew we was there because I could hears all the noises that I hads heard before. It wasn't long before we droved onto the boat. Mum cames into the back with me as soon as we stoppsed.

"Okay Jasper, we have to leave you and go upstairs for the boat trip, but it won't be long and I will put some of your favourite music on. We will be back soon."

They gaves me a big kiss and a cuddle and then closed the door as they left. At firsts all the noises and hooman shoutings did gives me the uneasies, but my tinkly music mades me calms and of courses, I hads my hay. The trip was really quicks actually, a lots quicker than the other trips I had beens on. Before I knews it, the lorry side door opened.

"There see, I told you it wouldn't be long," Mum said as she was giving me some cuddles. I really likes cuddles.

As we droves off the boat, I could see through the window that it was dark outsides and I hads no idea where we was going, but Mum and Dad were with me, so I was feelings very calms about it all. The drive was really short thanks the goodness because the boat and now the lorry was starting to makes me feels really squeezy. We soon cames to a stop and when the door opened again, I could sees a big barn with lots of stables inside, filled with big horses. As I hobbleds down the slope of the lorry and limped into the barn, I prepareds myself for the usual comments abouts my size from the big horses, but much to my surprises, it didn't happens. In facts they were very nice, although some of them spokes funny.

"Bomb door," some of them said as I passed. Don't know whats they were on abouts, but they saids it very nicely.

"Hello, nice to meets you," another one said.

"Hello, I'm Jasper."

"Oh you poor pony, what's happened to you?" Asked a very tall, black mare.

I was just about to answers, when I was putted into

a very bigs stable, with a pile of the greenest, bestest hay, I hads ever seeds. I totally forgots about the funny speaking horses and their questions.

"I likes this France," I said to myselfs as Mum putted my pyjamas on and tucked me in.

"Night, night my gorgeous boy," Mum said as she gaves me a big kiss. "See you in the morning."

"Thanks Mum. Loves you," I said, still eatings.

When the hoomans left to goes into the big house, all the horses in the barn started asking me lots of questions, but first I needed to knows where I was.

"So is this the hospital then?" I asked the horse closest to me. I could just sees his head through the bars above me. These stables weren't like mine at home because the sides were all wood, so I couldn't really sees out.

"Nope, it's just where Jersey horses come to stay before the drive up there. You will go in the morning," said the tallest, shiniest horse, I had ever seens.

"Oh," I said. "Why do the horses on that side of the barn keeps saying, "bomb door to me? Is they being rudes?" The big horse laughed so louds, it mades me jump and I hurted my shoulder.

"Oh sorry Jasper, I didn't mean to make you jump. They were saying hello in French. You are in France

43

you know," he said still chuckling.

"It's not bomb door either, its bonjour," he said. "You might want to learn some French, if you are going to be staying a while."

"Why don't you speaks funny likes them?" I asked.

"Most of us come from England, like the hooman that owns us. We are her horses. The ones on that side of the barn have been sold and will be leaving for Jersey very soon."

"I see," I said fascinated by it all. I spent the whole night chattings with them, tellings them about my adventures. I cided that France is a very friendly place and I quite likes it. I even learnts some French words. How clever am I?

The next morning a very nice lady hooman cames out and gaves me my breakfast and another big pile of the lovely green hay. I was so happy eatings that I didn't notice Mum comes into my stable. She got me all brushed and outs of my pyjamas and before I had times to finish all my hay, I was back on the lorry. I has to admit, I was quite sads to leaves that place.

It was quite a long drives to the hospital, but I hads someone to talks too, so it wasn't too bads. When we gots there, Mum opened the big door, so I could gets some fresh air. I can't tells you how hot it is in the France.

I had a nice drinks of cold water and I had a goods look around. There were lots of other lorries comings and goings and lots of horses getting on and offs.

"What a busy hospital this is?" I thoughts to myself. I suddenly realized that Mum had disappeared, but just as I was abouts to get the worries, I seed her walksing over with another lady hooman. They were chattings away, about me I thinks.

"Hi Jasper, my name is Philappina and I am going to look after you whilst you are here," she said.

Next minute she was kneeling downs next to me giving me big cuddles, I likeds her rights away. A pony can tell you know, if a hooman is nice or not, by the way they feels when they gives you the cuddles. Mum leaded me offs the lorry and I was alloweds to stop on a lovely grassy patch. French grass tastes as good as their hay. I was so busy with the munching, I didn't hears Dr. Ro arrives until she gaves me the big hugs. She really loves me you know. She loves me so much, she broughted her mum to meets me. Don't thinks I has ever hads so many kisses and cuddles from so many hoomans.

There were lots of very big horses at the hospital and I don't think they were happy to sees me. They certainly didn't seems very impressed that I was having so much of the hooman attentions. Just when I was starting to feel nice and relaxed, Philippina took my lead rope and walksed me inside a very big room that was a bit darks. There was lots of hoomans in there and they were all starings at me. I am not going to lie, I suddenly felts a bit afeared. I quickly looksed for Mum and pulleds away from Philippina and hids behind Mums legs.

"Mum, I thinks I have seens enough of this hospital," I said.

She knelt down and did the whisperings in my ear. "Don't be scared, I'm not leaving you and it will all be over soon. Be brave sweetie," she said as she handed me back to Philappina.

Another lady hooman, who looksed very importants, cames over and talksed to Dr. Ro and they hads the big chats about my shoulder. I just kept looksing at Mum because I knew if I could sees her, I would be okay. There were lots of hoomans around me now and one of them was tying my mane up.

"What are you doings?" I said with the irritations. Then it happened! One of the hoomans stuck me with a prickly stick in my neck and befores I had the times for the panics, I felt all dizzy and woozy.

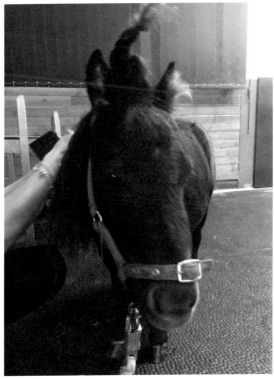

"Mum! What's happening? I'm feeling squeezy!" I shouted. I couldn't moves and I was full of the fuzzies, but I could just sees this big machine coming downs on top of me. I really wanted to goes home now, I changed my minds about the France. It didn't ends with the machines either because I heard a buzzy sound and I could feels the tingly over my shoulder. Next thing I felts was some cold sticky stuff being put on it and a slidey thing goings backwards and forwards. Actually I didn't minds that bit. Just as I was starting to get the relaxations, another lady hooman, stuck another, even bigger prickly stick in my shoulder. I heard Dr. Ro tellings mum it was a stairwoid. Apparently it would takes the pain aways. Lets me tells you, it certainly didn't takes away the pain of it goings in. I had really hads enough of it all and the fuzziness was starting to goes away, so I managed to find the strengths to pull away and runs to Mum.

"I needs to go home now. Please can we goes? I don't likes it here anymores?" I said with the big upsets.

Mum sat on the floors with me and gaves me some cuddles and trieds to make me feels better. Thanks the goodness, she leaded me outside, so I could have a bit of grass. Dr. Ro cames with us and they had the big chats about my shoulder. It seems I did breaked it, just likes I saids, but now I have had the stairwoid prickly stick, I should be better in no times at all, Dr. Ro saids.

I stayed outs on the grass for a longs time in the sunshines, which did makes me feels a lot better. I didn't looks up until Dr. Ro cames over to say goodbye. She gaves Mum and me the big hugs and then she left. Lots of hoomans cames over to sees me. Apparently, they has never had a pony as small as me at the hospital, so everybody wanted to takes my pictures. You might not knows this, but I am quites famous in the France. I thinks I was just as famous with all the horses too because they were all stood in a row, looksing at me over the fence. They didn't says a word either, just stoods starings at me.

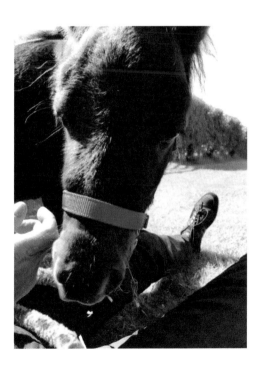

"Right Jasper, it's time for your rest now," Philappina said. She showed us to a lovely big wooden house with lots of stables in it. There was a funny smell comings out from it, that I didn't likes very much. Smelled likes medicines to me. As we walksed down to my stable, I seed lots of horses, some looksed very sick and some just looksed very afeared. In facts, just looksing at them gaves me the uneasies. By the times I reached my stable, I had flutterflies in my tummy. Dad cames and sat with me, whilst Mum and Philappina had the chats about my foods.

Dad putted my pyjamas on and tolds me they hads to go, but they would be backs in the morning to collects me. Can't tells you how happy I was to hears that, but I wasn't happy when I saw the very small pile of hay Philappina hads given me.

"Excuse me, I thinks you have forgotten the rest of my hay. Hello! Philappina!" I shouted as loud as I coulds. "Well this won't do," I thoughts to myselfs. Just as I was abouts to have the panics, Mum and Dad creepted back into my stable with a lovely full haynet. "You reads my mind," I said.

Mum quickly hanged it up and whispered in my ears. "I don't think they know how much you like your hay Jasper. Can't have you going hungry can we."

I gaves her the biggest kiss and breathed a big sigh of the reliefs. I can handles anything, if I has the hay. When I gets hungry, it reminds me of the nasty place and that just makes me feels sads.

It was a long night and I didn't get much of the sleeps, on accounts of the groaning and moaning coming from the horse in the stable next to mine. I did asks if he was alright, but he was French and the only words I knows hows to say are, "bomb door and mercy", which means hello and thank you, if you didn't knows. Don't think he was in the moods for the talksing anyways.

Mum and dad arriveds very early the next day, just after breakfasts, they packed up my pyjamas and gotted me back on the lorry. I can't say I was sad to leaves. Hospitals are not the nicest of places I has scovered, full of the sickness and the prickly sticks.

The drive back to the boat tooks a very long time, but Mum and Dad kepts talksing to me through the window, to checks I was okay. I must say my shoulder was definitely feelings better. I was just desperates to get backs to Teddy and Buddy. I was even missings Gizzy, which filled me with the surprises.

When we gots to the boat place, I actually felt the comforts when I heards all the noises. I was gettings used to it all now and the way I looksed at it, the boat was goings to takes me home, so I was glads of it. It was quite a longs time before we loaded and it was very hot, so Mum hads to open up the doors, so I could cools down. I drank loads of the waters she putted in a bucket for me and I has to say, I was very pleased when we finally droves onto the boat because it was nice and cool.

"Right Jasper, see you in a bit, we have to go upstairs like last time, but we will see you when we get to Jersey," Mum said.

"It's okay mum, I wills be fine. See you laters," I said munching on my hay.

I don't know why but the boat trip back seemed quicker somehows, before I had times for a lie down, they were backs.

"We are here Jasper, you will soon be back in your stable," Mum said.

I thinks they were just as pleased as me to gets home and thanks the goodness, the drives back was quick. As soon as the lorry stopped on my grassy patch, I could hear Teddy shoutings to me.

"He's home, he's home. Gizzy, he's home. HELLO JASPER!" Teddy shouted.

He carried on shoutings until I reached his stable. I went straights up to him and gaves him the hugs, mostly to stops him shoutings, but also because I was just as pleased to sees him.

"Hello Teddy, hello Gizzy. I really missed you all," I said. I was going to sticks my head up to Gizzy, but then I changed my minds, I don't think he is quites ready for that. I trotted into my stable as quick as I coulds, to say hello to Buddy, who was running around my stable full of the excitements.

"Jasper I have really missed you. Is your shoulder all better now?" he asked.

"It feels a lot betters Buds and guess what? I can goes back on my grassy patch!" We all stayed ups most of the night, so I could tells them all abouts my trip. Teddy was very interested in the French hay, especially when I tolds him, it was the greenest, sweetest hay, I hads ever tasted.

53

"Oooh! I would really likes to try some of that. I wish Mum had brought us some back," he said.

We did eventually falls asleeps. Teddy was dreamings about the French hay. He talks in his sleeps you know. Gizzy says it fills him the annoyances. I thinks lots of things fills Gizzy with the annoyances.

Life got backs to normals afters my French adventure and I loved being out on my grassy patch everyday. Teddy was full of the disappoints that I couldn't go in withs him and Gizzy. Mum said she couldn't risks me hurting my shoulder, before it gots all better and we all knows I can be a naughty pickle. I can't helps it.

CHAPTER 5

Now, you would thinks this would brings me to the end of my story, but nothings is ever that simples in my lifes. You sees, my shoulder wasn't my only problem. Apparently, my bones haves growed funny and Dr. Ro thinks it was either something that happened when I was in my mothers tummy or because of the starving I hads from the nasty farmer. Anyways, it meant that I was on my tippy toes alls the times. I gets a bits fused abouts the why. I thinks it's the springy things that holds my bones togethers, couldn't keeps up with the ways my bones were growing and that's why my feets were going on tippy toes. The elastics are too shorts! So Mum hads to call Dr. Ro to comes and takes a look because my feets were getting worserer and worserer.

"Oh no!!! Why is Dr. Ro here? Please don't let it be me. Please don't let it be me." Teddy kept saying over and over.

"Teddy, its not you, so just stop!" Gizzy said.

Dr. Ro spent ages taking pictures of my legs and yes, I hads to have the sleepy prickly stick. Everything was a bits fuzzy, so I could only just hears was Dr. Ro was saying to mum, but I definitely heards somethings abouts going into hospital. My tummy gots the flutterflies and I suddenly felt squeezy. I don't knows what they were thinking, I means, I can gallops faster than Ted. I is fines!

The next couple of weeks were alls abouts the hospitals trip. I hated it and I could tells that Mum and Dad were full of the worries. I really didn't want to goes this time and I tried to tells Mum that I wasn't going to get on that lorry when the times came, but she wasn't listening to me.

"But why are you going again Jasper? I thought you said your legs were all better?" Asked Teddy.

"I has no ideas, I am nots going to go, so don't you worries. I am feds up with alls this leg busyness. I just fuse to go and that's that." I went and stood with Buddy and tried not to thinks about it all and I showed Mum how full of the annoyances I was. I hads the grumps right ups until she tried to leads me onto the lorry. I fused to go on, but Dad just lifted me up and carpied me. Full of the shocks I was, how rudes is that? I has no digsnity, I tells you. Why wasn't I borns with the longer legs? You don't sees big horses being carried anywhere, do you?

At first I was full of the uneasies, but then I thoughts, this is happenings whether I likes it or not, so I might as well makes the best of it. The trip to the boat was short likes last time, but the boat trip to the England tooks a very long time and I has to say that the noises seemed louder and more scaries. When we finally arrives, it was dark and we hads a very long drive before we finally stopped again. I thought it would be like the last times I was in hospitals in France, but this place was different.

When I was finally takens out of the lorry and leaded to my stable, everybody was very sewious and I didn't get any hellos or cuddles from the hoomans. There was no Philappina at this hospital. I suddenly felts very afeared and so I stopped suddenly, with the hopes that if I fused to walks to the stables, I coulds go back on the lorry. I hads to gives in though because I am just too smalls to gets my owns way and the hooman in charge of things didn't looks very impressed with my antiques. For some reason she didn't gets my cutesness.

I didn't likes my stable either, it was very dark, but at least I hads a sees through door, although what I seed didn't fills me with the comforts. The horse that was facing my stable was the hugest horse I hads ever seeds and he was full of the grumps. He had a big bandage around his neck and he was doing the groaning. He really freaksed me, so I tries not to looks at him. None of the other horses were talksing and none of them saids hello to me.

"Mum, I has cided this isn't the place for me. I thinks we should leaves right nows. Come on! Lets go quicks," I said full of the worries. Mum looksed as afeared as me and I don't thinks she wanted me to stay eithers, but no matter how much I asked and gaves my big loves you eyes, she didn't takes me away. Instead she putted on my pyjamas, gaves me a very big squeeze and said she would be back in the morning. Not goings to lie, I hated it and I didn't wants to stay, but I thoughts, maybe its just for one sleeps. I waited for my hay because the hay always makes me feels better, but when it arrived, I hads the flutterflies again.

It was the smallest bit of hay, even lesses than what Philappina gaves me in the France. I waited for Mum to brings me my owns hay from home, likes last time, but she didn't comes. They wouldn't lets her. I was full of the sads and I just quietly eated my little bits of hay and tried not to looks at the scary horses. I didn't gets much sleeps on accounts of my tummy rumbles, but at least I gots the breakfast. Then, thanks the goodness, Mum and Dad arriveds. "Is we goings home now? " I asked.

She didn't answers me and before I had times to do more pleases, some hoomans came, which I heard mum say were my doctors. They took me out of my stable and I walksed very slowly at firsts, as I wasn't sures where they was taksing me. Then Mum handed me over to a doctor and they said I hads to do the trots up the road. Well, that's when I seed my lorry, so I thoughts, okay hoomans, I has hads enough. I did the gallops and dragged the doctor behinds me, all the way up the path to my lorry. For some reasons, she and all the other hoomans thought it was very funnies. I don't knows why, I thinks this was all very sewious. Very sewious indeeds.

Well she broughted me back and I hads to do the trotting ups and down, which really filled me with the annoyances. I was prodded and poked for ages and I wasn't offereds one singles carrot, cans you believe? When they was finished, Mum and Dad cames over.

"Mum, I am full of the disappoints with you. I thinks we needs the words. You is sposed to looks after me you knows!" I said. Much to my surprises, she didn't says the sorries. Instead she gaves me more of the bad news.

"Rights my lovely boy, we have to leave you now because we're not allowed to stay for the next bit, but we will be back later to see you. Be brave," she said as she gave me a big kiss and a cuddle.

"Why do I needs to be braves? What's happenings? You can't leaves me with these hoomans." I shouted as they tooks me away. I was really afeared now. They tooks me into a big room that was quite dark and it had lots of big scary things in it, but before I could do anythings about it, I hads the sleepsy prickly stick.

Doctors really likes givings the prickly sticks. I wasn't really sures what was happenings, but they used the big machines likes I had in the France. When they was done, they tooks me back to my stable. I didn't haves any hay and I was feeling very squeezy. Thanks the goodness Mum cames back to sees me and I heards her talksing to the doctors. I was going to haves an opseration the next day to cuts somethings. Well, I hads the panics when I heards that.

"I am havings the what done, to my whats?" I asked anyone that was listening to me. Mum didn't answers, she was still talksing to the doctors.

Then for the first time since I arrived the huge, grumps horse, opposites me spoked. "You are having your legs cut off tomorrow," he said.

I didn't moves, I just stareds at him. I couldn't evens swallows, in facts, I thinks I stoppsed the breathing. Mum bent downs and gaves me the cuddles, which was good because I thinks I was abouts to falls over. I couldn't talks, I was in the shocks.

"Lets go for a walk in the sunshine," Mum said as she putted my rope on. "Yes, I needs the walks, after alls, I might never walks again!" I said with the grumps. We walksed behind all the stables and we founds a nice grassy patch for me too eats. With all the shocks, I hads forgotten how hungry I was. Whilst I was eating and did I eats, Mum explained that I was going to haves an opseration to cuts the elasticky things in my legs, so that my feets woulds be right again. She said it wouldn't be that bads and I would be all betters afters. To be quites honest, I wasn't really listening because I was more interested in the grasses. I was so hungry and I hads a feeling, I wasn't goings to gets much hay laters.

We spent the whole afternoons on the grassy patch and I has to say I was not happies to go back to my stable, but I did and at least I hads the full tummy.

Mum gaves me my night time brush and putted my pyjamas on and lefts me again. She was doings that a lots lately. The grumps horse didn't speaks to me again eithers, which was good because I did haves the worries abouts this opseration I was goings to have.

Mum and Dad cames back in the morning, just before I gots another prickly stick and I wasn't feelings very braves. "Please don't go, don't leaves me with these hoomans. They don't likes me and what if they tries to cuts my legs off," I said to Mum.

She just gaves me the hugs and said, "We will come back later sweetie. I love you."

My tummy was really full of the flutterflies now and I thinks it was the most afeared I has ever been. Thanks the goodness, I had the sleepsy prickly stick, straights away. Never thoughts I would says that.

When I awoked from the sleeps, I was backs in my stable and I felts really sore. I quickly looksed down at my legs, to makes sure they were still there. I was so reliefed to sees them, even though they were stiffs and hads the bandages wrappeds arounds them. "Hello, my lovely legs." I said looksing down at them. I went to walks. "What is goings on with these legs, why aren't they doings what I is tellings them to?" I said, to myselfs. I felt something biting my neck too and I could sees that the sames stuff that was around my legs, was wrapped arounds my neck. "I don't likes this. I don't likes this at all." Then I seed that I hads these pink socks on my feets. "What on the earths is goings on?" Then to my reliefs, I seed a small piles of the hay nears my water bucket. Alls of a sudden, I forgots abouts my weirdy legs, funny socks and my soreness.

"Okay legs, we has to makes it over to the hays." I hads to move really slowly and sort of jiggles my way across my stable. It tooks a very long times, but I mades it and I stuffed as much hay as I could in my mouths. "I loves you hay," I said.

Mum cames to visit later, but to be honests, I wasn't my bestest self. I just really wanted to goes home to Teddy, Buddy and Giz. "Can we goes now?" I asked as soon as Mum cames in.

She looksed full of the sads when she seed me and I am not surpriseds because I looksed diculous. I hads bandages arounds my legs with sticks inside, so I couldn't bends them, bandages arounds my neck and the silliest pink socks on my feets. I would haves been full of the embarrassments, if I wasn't so sores.

"I needs the hugs mum. Looks what they has dones to me!" I saids, feelings very sorries for myselfs.

Mum and Dad gaves me lots of cuddles and talksed to me, which did makes me feels a bit better, but they weren't taksing me home. They visited again the next morning and that's when they saids it. The worstest thing they could ever says to me.

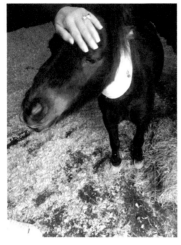 

"Now Jasper, we have to go back home to look after Teddy and Gizzy but you need to stay here for an extra couple of weeks. When your legs are all better, we will come back to get you. It will go really quick, I promise." Mum said with the leaksy eyes. Dad was full of the upsets too.

I thoughted my heart would breaks. I really didn't want to stay and I definitely didn't wants to stay withouts Mum and Dad. But they did leave and things got worserer. I hads hardly any hay because they said I was too fats, which is very rudes I thinks and then they tolds me, I hads to have another opseration because the first one didn't goes right. I hads to stay there five weeks instead of the two. It was the worstest five weeks of my lifes. The hoomans were too busy, so I hads no cuddles and the horses and ponies that I could sees, didn't want to talks to me. I was very lonely. Each day I just stoods on my own and waited for my little bits of hay. I really started to thinks that maybe Mum and Dad had forgottens about me and that I would haves to stay here forevers. I am not goings to lie, I did gets full of the depressions.

The doctors cames in and gaves me medicines and wrapped new bandages around my legs, but I just stood there, fulls of the emptiness and the sads. I just switched my feelings off. Now I knew why all the other horses hads the grumps. They had been here longers than me.

Then one morning as I waiteds for my hay, I thoughts I was dreamsing because I could hears Mum and Dads voices. I didn't looks up because I thoughts it wasn't reals, but then I felts someone cuddlings me and then I heards her voice.

I looksed up slowly at first, but then I seed her. "Mum, Mum, you're backs, you're backs. I loves you and I has really missed you," I said, as I jumped on her with the excitements. I kissed her, all overs her face. "I thoughts you had forgottens me." I couldn't believes they were here.

"Jasper you look so skinny," she said.

"Mum, you has no ideas what I has been though in this place. No hay, no cuddles. It's been terribles!" I said.

They tooks me out to the grassy patch and we spent the whole day togethers and then I was already to leaves.

"You just have to stay for one more sleeps, I promise, " Mum said.

"Okay, but I will not stays one days longer. I has hads enough of this place."

The next morning, just after breakfast, they cames just as Mum promised. They packed up my pyjamas and leaded me out of my stable. As you knows, I don't likes going onto the lorries and Dad normally has to carries me on, but this time, even with my sore legs, I gallopsed onto that lorry. I has never been so happies to leaves a place in all my lifes. Mum and Dad thought it was larious.

CHAPTER 6

The trip to the boat was long and very bumpy, but I didn't care, I was going home. I just eated as much hay as I could fits in because I hads been so hungry for such a longs time. I didn't evens notice Mum leaves me on the boat or all the noises. It was a long trip and I was glad when they comes back and tolds me we was finally in the Jersey. Best thing I has ever heards.

As soon as we arrives at my grassy patch, I could hears Teddy. He was screaming his head off. "It's Jasper, it's Jasper!"

Well, as soon as I gots off the lorry, I wents as fast as I could to gets to my bestest friends in the whole worlds. I gaves the biggest hugs to Teddy and even Gizzy looksed pleased to sees me. Buddy was just running around in the circles in my stable. "I can't tells you how much I has missed you all. I never wants to leaves you again. I really loves you," I said.

"We really missed you too Jasper and we don't want you to leave again either," Ted said.

Mum settled me into my stable with a lovely big haynet and some carrots. I tooks a big deeps breath and looksed at my family and I felts so happies. Then I looksed at my new fluffy bed, "Hello bed, I missed you too." We all stayed up talksing all night and I tolds them all abouts my terribles time at the hospital. They couldn't believes what had happeneds to me.

The next morning, when Dad cames out to gives us our breakfast, he seed that my leg was all fat. "To be honests with you Dad, it is feelings a bit squidgy," I said. Dr. Ro cames up to has a looks and she saids that the second opseration had caused the problems and now the liquids in my legs wasn't movings properly. I don't sees how that happeneds because I don't drinks a lot really.

I hads to have the bandages on again, which I didn't likes much. Very hots and itchy they are. Thanks the goodness, I was still alloweds to go on my grassy patch. I thinks I missed my grassy patch as much as I missed my family. I had a good trot about when I gots in there. "Hello bunnies, hello beaksy birds, I am backs," I shouted full of the happies.

My legs stayed puffy for months and then they wents very wonky and I means crazy wonky. Dr. Ro saids she hads never seed anything likes it. Well, I am not a doctor, but if they cutted my elastics, of courses they is going to go wonky. There is nothings holdings them up! I tolds Dr. Ro, "Why is you full of the surprises. I hads the elastics for a reason you knows."

Everybody hads the worries abouts it. I hads all sorts of things done and then Mum gots some braces mades for me, in the California. That's in the America you know. Got to say, they was the ugliest things I had ever seeds and they didn't feels good eithers. "I is very sorries, but I is not going outs with these on. I looks diculous and they feels too tights. Looks! I can't walks," I said, with my legs swinging out sideways.

I dids get used to them in the ends and they were helpings a bit. Dr. Ro saids, that my elastics that holds my bones straight, were all loose. I said, "I tolds you that already." I don't gets why they just don't tightens them up. Mum does it with my coats all the times, although lately, she seems to be loosenings them, rathers than tightenings them. Apparently I is a bit rounds for my size. Personally, I thinks I looks just fine and I do needs to keeps my strengths up.

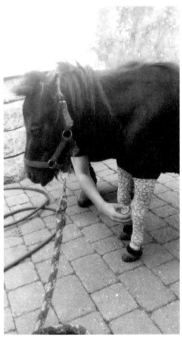

Whilst all this was goings on, poor Gizzy gots the sickness because his feets gots trimmed wrongs and it mades the bottoms too thins. He was so lame and very sores. He hads to have lots of the time in his stable, likes I had. Teddy was full of the upsets. Gizzy was his bestest friend ever since he arriveds sixteen years ago and after losing his lovely Honey, he hads the real worries. So when we were in the grassy patch, I thoughts I would tries and cheers him up.

"Gizzy will be fines Ted, looks at me, I have hads everythings happens to me and I is alrights," I said.

"You are too young to understand Jasper. When I first came here I had a big family and we all looked after each other. They made me feel safe. They have all gone now and I only have Gizzy left. I don't know what I will do if I lose him too."

"But you has me and Buddy, we loves you." Nothing I said made Teddy feels better, all he wanted was Gizzy to be back outs with him again.

Mum tried everythings to gets Gizzy well, but nothing would work and now he had the Laminitis, so he was in a lots of pain. He is the bravest pony, I has ever knowed because he never moaned or plained abouts it. Gizzy didn't talks much about his time before coming here, but Teddy said he had awful things done to him. He wouldn't let a hooman go nears him and he was afeared of everything. He had been passed from one home to anothers and some nasty ones at that. Horses and ponies really goes throughs it you know. All we wants is a kind forevers home, but most of us aren't lucky enough to gets that. It tooks Mum and her bestest friend who I calls Aunty Lizzie, a longs time to gets him to trust hoomans again and now he does, although only family hoomans. He said this is the first proper home he hads ever had and he was so happy when he founds out he would never be sold again.

"How is you feeling Gizzy?" I asked when I cames in from the grassy patch.

He didn't answers me, he just stood at the back of his stable full of the miseries. Mum called DR. Ro out and she gaves him some strong medicines which made the pain goes away for a bit. I heards her telling Mum that there was nothing more she could do, as it had turned into a viral Laminitis that was gettings worserer by the minute. Then I heards Dr. Ro says it. "I am really sorry, but the kindest thing to do, is put Gizzy to sleep."

Mum was full of the upsets and I seed Dr. Ro giving her the hugs. I had the right shocks when I heards them says that it would happens the next morning. My tummy started doing the turns and I felts full of the upsets. How would I tells Teddy and what could I do to helps everybody? Gizzy and me weren't bestest friends, but I loveds him. Thanks the goodness, I didn't haves to tell Teddy anything because Gizzy had heards her too and he tolds him what was going to happens.

I was specting a night of the sadness, especially from Teddy, but Gizzy was happy and talksing about the good times he hads here with the horses and ponies that had already gone to the forevers place. Even Teddy was enjoying talksing about the things they used to gets up to.

"Do you remember Ted, when you first came and you were in stallion mode. I couldn't believe my eyes when I saw you try and climb on Max. Jasper you should have seen him. That horse was a giant and Max couldn't work out what Teddy was trying to do. Teddy couldn't reach further than the back of his legs," Gizzy said laughing his head off. "How he didn't get kicked, I will never know."

We all laughed. Apparently, Teddy was quites the handsful, when he was a colt. I couldn't imagines Teddy being likes that because he is always so sewious and growed up now. Gizzy went on to talks about his time at the shows with Chloe, that's Mum's daughter hooman. They won everything togethers they did. It sounded likes so much funs. Then Gizzy went quiets.

"I know you are all worried about me, but I don't want you to be. It's my time and I am ready. Mum said she will stay with me and she will help me go across to the forever place. Our family will meet me there. Ted I will see Aslan, Honey, Mootie, Max and even Lancer. I am really looking forward to seeing them all again and best of all, I will be pain free. I can gallop again and eat grass all day, everyday. It's a good thing. I don't want you to miss me and Teddy, I want you to look after Jasper. I am leaving you in charge now," he said in the kindest voice.

"I will Gizzy, I will, I promise, but don't ask me not to miss you because I will." Teddy said before walksing over to his stable door. He spent ages, just looksing out. I wondered what he was thinksing.

It was a long night and none of us sleepsed. We just didn't wants the light to comes because we knew we would haves to say goodbyes to Gizzy and I knews that would be the hardest thing in the worlds for Teddy. But it did comes and I am sures it was quicker than normals. None of us eated our breakfast and we was all very quiet.

Mum cames and got Gizzy really early, just as the sun cames up and tooks him to our grassy patch. I can't tells you how exciteds he was to be back out again. Mum wanted him to spends some nice quiet time eatings and watching the sun comes up. Mum and Dad stayed with hims the whole time and I wished I coulds have been there too. Teddy wouldn't talks, he just stood at the back of his stable with his head hangings down. I didn't says anything because I didn't knows what to says.

I heard Dr. Ro arrives and soons after that, I seed mum run past my stable with the upsets. Well that set Teddy off because we knew Gizzy was gone.

"Teddy, I is here, I won't leaves you and remember what Gizzy saids, you mustn't be sads, you has to be happy. He has gones to a specials place with your family. Please be okays because I don't thinks I will handles things if you aren't."

Teddy didn't answers me, so I just stood with Buddy.

I can't remembers how long we all stoods like that, but eventually Dad took us out to our grassy patch. Teddy went over to where Gizzy laid asleeps under the grounds and I followeds close behind. Teddy just stared down.

"You were my best friend Gizzy and I will never forget you," he said.

I didn't really knows what to do because I hads never known anyone who hads gone to the forevers place. I hads lots of questions which I couldn't ask Ted. Likes why was Gizzy in the ground? How would he gets to the forevers place? I thoughts I hads better ask mum abouts it all laters. I just kepted quiet and followeds Teddy. I hads to looks after him the best I coulds. Neither of us spoked for the rests of the day. Not going to lie, that was really hards for me because

78

you might not knows this but I really likes to talks.

Things were very quiets after that in the stables. Thanks the goodness I hads Buddy. Teddy just looksed into Gizzy's empty stable all the times.

CHAPTER 7

As the weeks went by, Mum had the worries abouts Teddy's depressions, so she tolds him that she was going to gets another friend to join us. A coloured pony from the England. His name was Mokey and he was eighteen months old. Teddy did cheers up a bits then, but he wasn't the sames and I had the worries that he never would be agains.

"What do you think he will be like Ted? I said. I was loosing forward to having someone new to plays with again. Especially after all the sadness. We needed some happy times.

"Let's hope he isn't like you," Ted said.

I was abouts to be full of the offences, when I seed that he was makings the fun. I was glads that he was a bits happier. Not longs after that Mokey arrived and cans you believes he is even smaller than me? We were all full of the excitements when he trotted up the drive. As soon as he gots into his stable, we started with the questions.

"So Mokey, where are you from? Were you nearly shooted and did Aunty Debbie rescues you?" I asked.

"I cames from a big grassy patch and I liveds with

all my pony family. I don't know what shooted is?" he said looksing a bit fused. "I have never been in a stable either."

I was abouts to tells him all abouts my lifes and what shooted means, when Teddy spoked. "Was it a nice grassy patch? I loves grass, " he said.

It was the firsts time since Gizzy left us, that I seed him looks happy. We all talksed, all through the night and by the morning, we were all good friends. We all went out to the grassy patch togethers, although I wasn't alloweds to plays with him at first on accounts of my legs. We had to all gets use to each others in our very own grassy patches. It was a good few days before Mum putted us in togethers.

"Listen Mokes," thats what I calls him. I only calls him Mokey when he is filling me with the annoyances, which is quite a lot actually, now I comes to thinks of it. "We has to be on our bestest haviour, otherwise Mum will keeps us seperates. We can plays when she isn't looksing," I said in the whispers.

"Oh, okay Jasper," he said.

I thinks our family was a bits of a shocks for him because he seemed a bit fused at firsts. We were really good, but then sometimes we couldn't helps it and we just played stallions until we were totally hausted. After alls, we are colts and that's what colts do. Mum noticed that playing with Mokes was actually making the elastics in my legs tighter, so she and Dr. Ro were full of the happies. Teddy joined in too sometimes, but he saids we were too excitables, so he asked to go on his own grassy patch for a whiles to haves some peace.

Mokes and me had the bestest time, we played stallions, we gallopsed and we eated. I has to say Mokey doesn't eats much, but I guesses that's because he has never been withouts the foods, likes me.

Things were really goods for a few months and we all thoughts I was over the worsts of my legs troubles, but then I wents really lame again. I hads to be in sorry tree confinesments. I hates that, but my legs were very sore. They started to go all wonky again, my heels started growing funny and my joints started to go all bendy. Mum trieds everything to gets me right. I hads the magnetic pulsey machines, the laser thingy, stairwoids and lots of other things that I won't goes into.

As I am writings this, I am waitings to have another opseration to cuts the elasticky things in my legs again. Thanks the goodness, I don't haves to go to the England hospital. The doctor is comings to the Jersey to do its, as Mum promised she would never takes me back to that hospital again. Dr. Ro and Mum says, that this opseration should fix things and afters I will finally be betters. Although I did hears them says that I has to haves the braces too, which I can tells you right now is not goings to happen. I don't do the braces.

So there you has it. I would have liksed to end this story with me being all wells again, playing with Teddy and Mokes in my grassy patch, but I don't knows when that will be yet. This does fill me with the frustrations, but what can I do? Sometimes you just haves to makes the best of things. Don't be sads for me because I is very happy. I has a lovely home, with the bestest family and I knows that I will be well soon. We all has to thinks positives and looks forwards.

Now, if you has enjoyed my story and you wants to stay in touch withs me, you can follows me on the Facebook. I writes a post everyday, keepsing you all updateds with my life and happenings and lets me tells you, there is always something goings on, especially with me beings the Grassy Patch Ranger. My Facebook page is "Jasper – Miniature Shetland Pony." I hopes you will joins me.

JASPER'S GLOSSARY

Afeared - Afraid

All moans – Hormones

Annoyances - Annoyance

Antiques – Antics

Beaksy Birds – Magpies

Bestest - Best

Bucksed - Bucked

Busyness - Busy

Calmsed – Calm or Calmed

Cided - Decided

Creepted - Crept

Depressions – Depressed

Diculous - Ridiculous

Digsnity – Dignity

Disappoints – Disappointed or Disappointment

Dreamsing - Dreaming

Droppsed - Dropped

Elastics – Tendons and Ligaments

Embarrassments – Embarrassed or embarrassment

Felled – Fell

Forevers Place – Heaven or Afterlife

Flutterflies - Butterflies

Freaksed - Freaked or Scared

Frustrations - Frustrated

Fused or fusions - Confused

Fuzzies – Dizzy or Dizziness

Gallopsed – Galloped

Grassy Patch - Field

Grumps - Grumpy or miserable

Happies – Happy

Hausted - Exhausted

Haviour - Behaviour

Heared - Heard

Hoodigan - Hooligan

Hooley - Wind

Hooman - Humans or people

Impresses - Impressed

Irritations – Irritated

Jiggled - Wriggled

Knewed - Knew

Leaksing - Crying

Leapsing – Rearing or jumping

Magnetic Pulsey – Magnetic Pulse Therapy

Monsooning – Raining

Opseratrion – Operation

Plained - Complained

Poppsed - Popped

Prickly Stick - Injection

Reliefed - Relieved

Sation - Conversation

Scaries - Scary

Scovered - Discovered

Seed - Seen

Sewious - Serious

Shooted – Shot

Sickness – Illness or Disease

Skitsy - Stressed

Sleepsed – Slept

Snapsed - Snapped

Smarts - Intelligence

Snugglesed - Snuggled

Sorry tree confinesment – Solitary Confinement

Specting - Expecting

Squeezy – Queasy

Squidgy - Swollen

Stairwoid - Steroid

Stoppsed - Stopped

Stopsing – Stopping

Taksing - Taking

Talksing – Talking

Tingly - Ultrasound

Tinkly Music – Nature Sounds Music

Uneasies - Uneasy

Walksing - Walking

Weirdy - Weird

Woofa - Dog

Worserer - Worse

PHOTOS

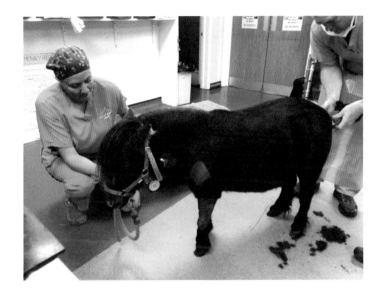

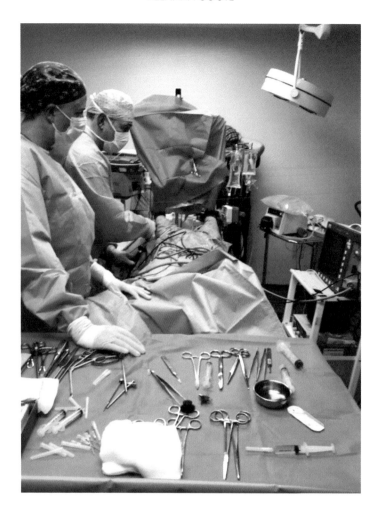

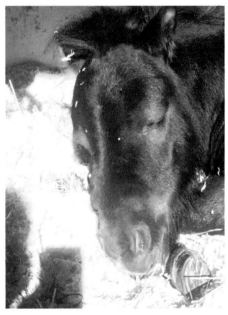

Printed in Great Britain
by Amazon